At Work in the Neighborhood

Leslie A. Rotsky

Sadlier-Oxford
A Division of William H. Sadlier, Inc.

Contents

There are people at work all over the neighborhood.

This person is a doctor.
She helps people who are sick.
Where does she work?

Turn the page.

She works at the hospital.

This person is a baker.
He makes bread and rolls.
Where does he work?

Turn the page.

7

He works at the bakery.

This person is a teacher.
She teaches reading and math.
Where does she work?

Turn the page.

She works at the school.

This person is a florist.
He grows and sells flowers.
Where does he work?

Turn the page.

He works at the flower shop.

This person is a mail carrier.
She delivers the mail.
Where does she work?

Turn the page.

She works all over
the neighborhood!

My Social Studies Project

Make a Riddle Card

What You Need:

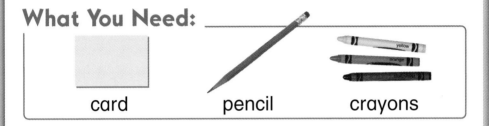

card   pencil   crayons

What You Do:

1. Choose a neighborhood worker.

2. On a card, write a "Who Am I?" riddle. Start by telling where you work. Then tell what you do. End with the question "Who am I?"

3. On the other side of the card, answer the riddle. Draw a picture of the neighborhood worker.

   I work in a bakery.

   I make bread and rolls.

   Who am I?

4. Share your riddle with a partner.

Index